OPENING DOORS

Poems by

Van Parker

OPENING DOORS

Poems by

Van Parker

Railroad Street Press
St. Johnsbury, Vermont

Copyright (c) 2012 by Van Parker

All rights reserved

Printed in the United States of America

Cover Design by
Susanna V. Walden

Front Cover Landscape Photograph by
Susanna V. Walden

Front Cover Door Photograph by
Minerva Studio

Back Cover photograph by
Lowell Fewster

LIBRARY OF CONGRESS
CATALOGING-IN-PUBLICATION DATA

_____

Parker, Van

ISBN 9781936711215

Railroad Street Press
394 Railroad St., Suite 2
St. Johnsbury, VT 05819

OPEN DOOR

After a dead end
It's quite amazing
To discover
An open door

For

My wife, Lucille (Lucy)
Our children, Susan, Beth and Doug
Their spouses, Ann, George and Kim
And grandchildren, Beth Nargi , Grace, Luke
and Jamie Murnaghan,
Maddie, Jackson and Faith Parker

ACKNOWLEDGEMENTS

I would like to express my thanks to:

Wayne Rollins, Gretchen Skelley and Bob Szostak for helping me arrange the poems in this book.

Lowell Fewster for the picture on the back cover.

David Budbill and Rennie McQuilkin for counsel on writing poems.

My wife, Lucille, for her encouragement and practical wisdom.

Thanks also for the poets who have unknowingly influenced me, and for friends who say simply "keep on writing."

OPENING DOORS

TABLE OF CONTENTS

PART ONE
SEASONS

PART TWO
WEIGHTY MATTERS

PART THREE
CREDO

PREFACE

When I was in my late teens my mother gave me a book containing the collected works of Robert Frost. He was at the time and in many ways still is my idea of what a poet should be like. But writing poetry never "took" with me until I turned 80. As though to make up for lost time, I've been writing poems ever since!

Diving into poetry hasn't brought up any answers to the deeper "why?" questions. But I am discovering that poetry can open doors and let in fresh air. Writing poems has helped me appreciate the amazing insight of psychologist Carl Jung. Jung believed that the unconscious is a very spacious place. It contains destructive elements. Yet it is also a place where Something can be discovered which binds people together and leads toward the highest good.

The prophet Jeremiah once asked an anguished question. "Is there no balm in Gilead? Is there no physician there?" A Spiritual, emerging from the nightmare of slavery, turned that question mark into an exclamation point. "There Is a Balm in Gilead, To Make the Wounded Whole!" I hope that among all the question marks in your experience you'll find, from time to time, an exclamation point.

Van Parker

PART ONE

SEASONS

BEGINNINGS

Beginnings are, most often,
inauspicious.
You hardly notice.
They rarely appear full-grown.
If, like the latest fashions,
they burst on the scene,
in most if not all cases
they deflate just as fast.
To see something new starting
you have to look in the
right direction
to find it,
not to some far off place
on the horizon
or heavenly vision.
Look at the ground,
as one looks
in late March or April or May
in a northern climate.
Rake off the old leaves.
Observe what's beneath them.
Look at the grass,
just starting to turn green.
Then at yourself and
the people you know.
Is something going on there?

SEED CATALOGUE

today I'm getting ready to order seeds
from the seed catalogue
a true rite of spring
beans, beets, lettuce, squash
that sort of thing

planting seeds is
a mysterious business
with luck and good weather
along with good wishes
seeds grow up to be
what they are, whatever
God made them to be
a little like people that way

wouldn't it be strange
and sort of unnatural
if a bean grew up
to be a tomato?

EARLY MORNING

This morning I saw
four pairs of cardinals,
a blue jay, assorted sparrows
and a junco.

In the midst of this assembly
of birds, two squirrels appeared.
One attempted to climb the pole
leading up to the bird feeder.
Defeated, it retreated
to a small patch of woods.

The other squirrel looked content
to gorge herself
with seeds that had spilled over
onto the bare ground.

The birds and squirrels
looked like they were
getting on well, or at least
staying out of each other's way.

None of them appeared bored
or at a loss as to what
to do next.

IN DEFENSE OF DANDELIONS

If there is such a thing as
re-incarnation,
I would like to take
a brief turn
as a dandelion.

This free-spirited flower
has no respect for
boundaries, seeding itself
indiscriminatingly
in lawns and fields

and in between cracks
in the sidewalk.
Efforts to get rid of it
show no signs of
long-term success

as the very next year,
in April or May,
there they are,
all those dandelions
with that bright
yellow smile

saying "Aren't you happy
to see us again!"

BLUEBERRY BUSHES

When we go north in the spring
the first thing I want to do
after unloading the car
is check out the blueberry bushes.

How did they manage the winter?
Are there dead branches to
prune? Will the weather be right?
Enough rain and sun
to keep them contented?

Blueberry bushes mature slowly.
They're a little bit shy,
requiring patience, pine needles,
sawdust – above all patience.

That small family of
fifteen bushes
can't be rushed or cajoled
or bullied.

They have their own
inner clock.
They're good teachers.

TREE TOUR

On a spring day toward the middle
of May I joined a walk with fifty or sixty
others in a place called Elizabeth Park.

Our guide told us the story of some of the
trees which grow in that park, highlighting
the leaves or needles and bark,

when these trees were planted,
where they originated, how high they
might grow, how long they could

live, whether they were hardwood or
softwood and their names
like Hornbeam, Weeping Blue Spruce,

Shagbark Hickory and Western Red
Cedar. Here they were, all in close
proximity, all seeming to get along

famously. What is it that draws a crowd
of various ages to those forty some trees
living harmoniously in a space of

less than a mile? In my case it was part
curiosity, part something else. Let's
say kinship with the fifty or sixty

people and with those various trees,
even one named Dawn Redwood
which has been around for 50 million
years, keeping company with dinosaurs
but not in this park, of course.

SPACE

Raspberries need space
the old man told me.
They don't like to be
crowded. I found the same
thing to be true for
radishes, carrots and beets.
The ones that prospered
had room to grow.

Are we so different
from the members of
the vegetable kingdom?
I don't think so.
"Don't crowd me"
we say.
"Back away"
"Stay out of my face"
"Give me some space"

BEACH AT HILTON HEAD

A late afternoon at the end of March
on a very warm day. Four of us were
walking along a beach at Hilton Head Island
and I found myself doing the following:

watching children building sand castles
and intricate designs in the sand,
avoiding marooned jellyfish,
noticing a small black dog dashing
in and out of the waves,

an expert kite flyer entertaining
beach goers by flying a kite over a
large expanse of water and sand,
a girl riding a bicycle along
the edge of the water.

Then, slowly, people starting to
pack up their belongings,
washing the sand from their feet.
Others stacking up piles of
beach chairs and umbrellas,
returning the beach to the seagulls,
shore birds and waves.

Don't know whether the tide was
coming in or going out
but walking along that beach
felt like an invitation to
be in touch with deeper tides,
and move from restlessness to rest.

BOTANICAL WONDER

In the middle of a botanical garden
filled with birds, bees, butterflies
and seasonal flowers of every
description, I came across

a large piece of petrified wood.
There it was,
right in front of me,
something reputed to be
90 million years old
but looking in very good shape.

It was a real tree when
dinosaurs were tramping around.
Then surviving in petrified form
when they disappeared.

I would like to have asked
some questions of this ancient specimen
of a tree:

– When did those dinosaurs disappear?
– Did cats and dogs show up soon after that?
– When did humans first appear?

I wished that stony tree could
give me a half hour to tell it's
story in an abbreviated way.

It didn't seem unapproachable
and the time would have passed
very quickly.

JUNE DAY

June is a month you don't want
To see go by too quickly
In these northern regions,
As it combines
    the freshness of spring
    and the warmth of summer.

A season of blooming roses,
Farmers harvesting the first
Crop of hay
And lupine blossoming in
North Country meadows.

A month for watching
Bean plants and lettuce as they
Spring out of the ground,
As though happy to
Arrive on the scene.

If you're lucky, June is long
On sunlight,
With enough rain to keep
Fields green and gardens growing.

June will go by
As every month does
And that's the more reason to
    smell the air
    feel the breeze
    stand on the ground

Enjoy it while it lasts.
All thirty days of it!
It won't be back
For another year.

HOLDING PATTERN

Another rainy day this June 24 in the Northeast
Kingdom of the State of Vermont
After a dry spell it's quite wet again.

No robins hopping around the lawn.
The birds must be hiding in trees and bushes.
Even the black flies have

taken their leave. Our field looks waterlogged.
Head high in some places, in others
nearly bent to the earth, waiting for the

first cut of the season. Seeds, planted a few
days back, still in the ground holding out
until the sun re-appears

which, according to the weather report,
will probably happen on
the day after tomorrow.

FOG

Sometimes, on a summer morning
In these hills, I notice that
The fog has moved in.

You can hardly see across the road
In front of our house, even though
The sun is already up.

The fog settles in for a while.
You can't wish it gone
And it goes.

But, often, by nine or ten A. M.,
It's gone.
The mountains, which of course

Were there all along,
Begin to appear, some of them
Forty miles away.

All you have to do
In this case
Is wait.

YEAR OF THE TOMATO

One year is not the same as another.
Certain things stand out
To make it distinct.

With that thought in mind
I'm taking the liberty of calling this year
The year of the tomato.

After a series of summers during which
Our tomato crop has hovered between
Disappointing and awful,

It's almost startling to see
Such happy and vigorous plants
Full of yellow blossoms turning into

Green tomatoes I can hardly believe
They're growing in the same ground
As their sad-looking predecessors.

      – No sign of tomato blight
      – Or branches turning brown
        And falling to the ground
        By the 4th of July

Could be that load of cow manure
Took hold. Whatever the cause
It makes you more hopeful

And not only about growing tomatoes
In the month of July
In this particular garden.

ONE RASPBERRY

On July 5 of this year
I walked down to the raspberry patch
To check on the berries
As I do most days this time of the year
To try to discover when those berries
Would be ready to pick.

There they were,
Thousands of berries, I think,
Though it's anyone's guess.
Yet not one that I could see
Ripe enough to eat.
Not until I came upon, at the end of my tour,

One almost ripe raspberry
Which could be eatable the very next day.
It seemed as though this lone ripe raspberry
Was sending a message which went
Something like this: "Try to be mellow
You impatient man

If you possibly can.
In a week or two there will be so many of us
You won't know what to do with us.
Plenty for cereal or pie or jam.
Enough to give to the neighbors.
By the end of this month or early the next

You might get sick of us."

RESTORATION

The old one room schoolhouse
hasn't been a school
nor its bell rung
in recent memory.

So the remounting of that bell
was a state occasion
in the midst of these hills
of North Danville, Vermont.

Neighbors had gathered
to see the crane lift that
700 pound unit and
put it back in its place.

They cheered and applauded
As three men on the roof
fastened it down securely
and as a woman

who went to school there
seventy-four years ago
went inside and
rang the bell once again.

ODE TO BEANS

If there is one vegetable
to which I am partial
it's beans,
both green and yellow.

I like to grow them
and eat them
and give them away.
They have a place of honor
in my garden.

Seven rows of them this year—
some blooming early,
some later.
We don't freeze them
or can them.

When their season is over,
we miss them.
It's not the same
to buy them
at the store.

RAIN

Rain today,
A good steady rain.
Just what was needed
According to the
Secretary of Agriculture
Of the state of Vermont.

Not a thunderstorm downpour
Or a quick passing shower
Or the kind of deluge
That makes gullies
In the dirt road
Which goes by our house.
But one that soaks into ground
That was getting thirsty.

Our field looks
Several shades greener.
The air feels cleaner.
Everything's fresher.
Almost like starting over
With a clean slate.

SEPTEMBER

I've never been able
To make up my mind
Whether September is an ending,
A new beginning,
Or a slow turning
As one season
Merges into another.

The garden's not growing
Except for some late lettuce.
Vacations are over.
The days slowly get cooler.

Some birds head south,
As do some people,
Including us.
In our case, not until October.

Pick-up trucks go by our house
And come back
Loaded with firewood
For the winter.

Is it a sad time,
A time of nostalgia,
This month of September?
Or is it a time in Northern
New England to enjoy the nip
In the air, to make a fresh start?
A little of both, I think.
But mostly the latter.

GIFTS GIVEN

This isn't a Christmas or a
birthday poem, or one about
occasions when, for whatever
reason, people give
or receive gifts.

It's simply a confession
that there are moments
when I become aware
of gifts that have been given,
some a long time ago.

Such moments can't be programmed
or written into a calendar.
They resist regimentation
and just appear,
welcomed but not planned for.

The gift of support, freely offered.
Unexpected kindnesses
from friends and strangers.
A wise word, nearly forgotten,
all of a sudden making sense

There they are, these unplanned gifts,
like the bright red leaves
of a red maple tree
across the valley
on a clear September day.

APPLE TREE

There's an apple tree in our yard
in North Danville.
No telling how old it is.
Looked old when we first saw it
forty- five years ago.
Must be a hundred by now.

Couldn't say what kind of
apple tree it is
or who planted it.
I've trimmed it once or twice.
Mostly it's on its own.

Every year it bears a crop
of maroon colored apples
which are good for apple sauce.

It keeps on bearing all
through the fall.
Then rests until spring.

HARVEST

Digging out carrots with a trowel.
Pulling up bean plants
And squash and cucumber vines
Plus various rows of lettuce
Which have bolted and
Aren't good to eat any more.

A pile of cucumbers in the kitchen
Which we eat for lunch and supper.
Broccoli, kale, swiss chard.
Zucchini in the refrigerator
Taking up space.
How long will it last?

How much shall we share
Of these vegetables?
How long will they keep?
How many can we eat?
A fleeting abundance
For which, I hope,
We are properly thankful.

Except for tomatoes, which
Didn't do very well.

PLAIN AS DAY

I don't believe poems should
leave you wondering
if you are qualified
to unravel their mysteries.

Wisdom and obscurity
don't necessarily go together.
Hidden meanings may not be there
to find.

Sometimes the truth of a matter
is in plain sight,
like the yellow maple leaves
 floating down outside the window

where I sit and watch them
on a suddenly bright
early October day.

TAKING OVER

Time to take down
 the old raspberry canes.
They've done their job,
yielded a good crop.

The new canes are
pushing them aside
as though wanting them
to get out of the way.

These upstarts will have
their time in the sun.
But they could be more
respectful as they take over.

TIRED

Been out in the vegetable garden.
Cleaning it up, as they say,
pulling out weeds, hoeing, raking.

It's good duty – clear air, box seat view
of the orange leaves
of a nearby maple tree.

But it's obvious the garden is tired.
Nurturing bean seeds, squash seeds,
swiss chard seeds,
cabbage plants, broccoli plants,
pepper plants – no easy job for this
small slice of Mother Nature.
Takes something out of her.

It's time to receive for a garden
that's been giving and giving
from spring to fall.
Time to be covered over with
maple leaves and cow manure.
Time to rest.

Spring will be coming
in six months or so.
No hurry for that.

AN INVENTORY OF LEAVES

This fall the leaves came off sooner than usual. By
early October they were mostly on the ground,
where they sit, or accumulate around the bushes.

Out here in the country no one uses leaf bags or
puts them out by the road to be picked up and
hauled to some anonymous leaf dump.

We're able to follow the leaves, to know more or
less what happens to them. You can, if you're so
minded, take an inventory of leaves. Which I did.

This year's inventory:

- some to fertilize the raspberry bushes
- some for the vegetable garden
- some to fill a hole in the driveway
- some back into the woods or ground

Leaves keep on working, if you let them.
They never retire.

NOVEMBER BEAUTY

A little starker,
a little plainer
than the month before it
or the month after.

Fields turning brown,
color fading,
if not already gone.
No more leaf tours
or chicken pie suppers
for north country visitors.

November is what it is,
a prelude to winter.
It ends with a holiday,
the least commercial,
most inclusive of any,
called simply Thanksgiving.

SOUTHERN LIVING

Our southern home is not very far south.
It isn't in Florida, Georgia or some
more temperate place.

It's in West Hartford, Connecticut,
200 miles south of Danville, Vermont
where we live in the summer.

It's a quiet place, sort of bucolic,
with wetlands on one side of it
and a park across the road.

Fourteen "cottages" inhabited by
eighteen people, last time I counted.
You have to be sixty-two to get in.

No hell raisers here. No wild parties
lasting into the night.
Most lights out by eleven or so.

We see deer now and then and bobcats
and foxes, keep track of our neighbors.
They call it Hartmeadow, after the deer.

It's like living in a refuge,
both for animals and people.

WINTER

It's winter here in Connecticut
and cold. Zero degrees Fahrenheit
when I checked at seven thirty
this morning.
Now it's gone up to eleven at quarter
of eleven
Plenty of snow on the ground.
They're predicting a record
amount for January.
The landscape looks frozen in place.

Plants and trees have hunkered down,
gone into hibernation,
biding their time, waiting.
Winter has a hidden quality
you've got to admire,
an incubator season,
made for reflection,
nurturing seeds and ideas.
All under the surface,
not yet visible.

NON WINTER

Let's just say that up until now
this has been an unusual winter
for the State of Connecticut.

No snow at all since twenty
inches of it fell
in the middle of fall.

Now here it is the
middle of January and
it's raining outside.
38 degrees Fahrenheit,
safely above freezing.

Has the snow all moved north
to the State of Alaska
where towns are reporting
fourteen feet of it?

What has happened to
the weather around here?
I'd settle for a few inches
of the white, fluffy stuff.
No ice, just snow.

reminding us of where
in the world we are, getting
matters back in order.
Not confusing the bulbs
in the ground, already
beginning to sprout.

How can poets write
poems about winter
when there's so little of it?

PART TWO

WEIGHTY MATTERS

WEIGHTY MATTERS

(With apologies to Meister Eckhart 1260-1327)

According to a man named
Meister Eckhart, the key to
a happier life
is in learning to let things go.

Like not staying angry at so and so
even if you think he or she is
a so and so,
or looking down at somebody else,
or trying to get even.

Learn to let go, Meister Eckhart
might say. Don't hold on to that
stuff. It's not what you've added
that makes you feel lighter.
It's what you've subtracted.

RESOLUTIONS

Resolution # 1

Slowly,
Over the years,
I've learned that
If you have nothing to say,
Don't say it.
Don't pretend
That you do.
Today
I have nothing to say
So I'll try
Not to say it.

Resolution # 2

Just look.
Be aware
Of what's around you,
How you might
Fit into the picture,
What you might do
Or not do,
Say or not say.
Then say it
Or do it.

RX

What works for one may not
for another but I would testify to the
therapeutic value of doing simple
things, like washing the dishes or
vacuuming the rug,

planting beans and lettuce,
talking to a neighbor, commenting on
the weather, letting your mind idle
in neutral, being surprised
by what comes to the surface.

These ordinary activities
could be remedies for trying to
become what you
weren't meant to be.

Find your own remedy or, if
you let it, it might find you.

FLOCK OF GEESE

On a wall in our dining room
is a picture of a flock of geese
standing in front of a barn,
all facing in the same direction.

They are domesticated geese
and stay close to home
not planning on migrating
to some distant place.

Are they lazy, these geese,
used to a life of ease?
Do they ever entertain
the possibility

they might end up
as somebody's supper?
I'd like to advise them to
get out while they can.

RUNNING OUT

One of the things
folks worry about
is running out,
as in running out of money
at the end of the month

or running out of time
to meet a deadline
or that one's health
could easily decline.

Is that why we rush around,
trying to capture whatever it is
that eludes us?

Have we missed springs
coming out of
the ground, bread provided
day after day,
as much as we need,

reminding us
the world is full of
renewable things.

ROUNDING THIRD

Baseball is an unusual sport.
Some find it boring.

Games have no time limit.
Unlike more fast- moving sports,
there are plenty of pauses.

Players often strike out.
One hit in three trips to the
plate is a very good average.

But there's something
about baseball
that speaks to the heart,

including the word home:
– home plate
– home run
– rounding third and heading for home.

Baseball is the only game
I know of where the goal is
to get back to where you started.

LIKE AN ANIMAL?

I would say that in many cases
comparing people who behave badly
to animals is an insult to animals.

If I were a dog or a horse,
a cow or a fox
and could put my
thoughts into words,
I would tell
the human species that
I was both hurt and offended.

Do these two legged creatures who
Think they're so smart
Know their place in the world?

And, if they do,
Might they learn,
At least on occasion,
To emulate us?

NATURAL

I wonder why some in the advertising business
spend so much time and money attempting
to make people look younger than they
happen to be.

This woman is fifty an ad proclaims.
Because of our skin cream she looks
twenty five. Sam is getting gray.
No doubt about it.
But you'd never know it.

Being safely on the far side of eighty
I feel free to comment on such matters.
Can't recall anyone saying "He's eighty-two
but doesn't look a day over
seventy-six."

After a while you're out of range of
the advertisers. Not in the market as
the saying goes. That lack of attention
may make you feel ignored but for the
most part it's great.

Being still alive I'd like to testify
that growing old and wearing
out is not something to waste time worrying
about. Sooner or later we move on.

The fountain of youth has never been found.
If it had, what would we do with all those
people hanging around?

QUESTION

Do people get wiser
as they get older?
Or just slower?

I wonder about that
from time to time.
There's some evidence

on both sides
of the matter.
Through luck, heredity

or whatever, older folks
are still alive.
They've seen fashions

come and depart.
Probably worked out
a few things.

But it might take them
a while to remember
what those things are.

INVITATION

Stop for a minute.
Take a break.
Don't do a thing.
Observe. Listen.
No need to prove a point,
Solve a problem.
Just be.

Watch the birds
Going about their business.
Look at the sunset
If it's not raining.
Yesterday, as the sun set,
Some of those clouds
Had a silver lining.

GREEN CHALLENGE

I'm fully supportive of
all things green
and in agreement with
scientists and climatologists
who say something must be done
about the world getting warmer.

I'd like, in some modest way,
to join other people
who want to
protect and reclaim
good old Mother Earth,
the ground and the air
and all the various species
sharing this planet.

It makes me feel good
to put in low watt light bulbs
and, when possible, to eat
food locally grown
and to recycle things

But it's still a challenge
to wash out an empty container
of peanut butter to the
degree that's acceptable
to the recycler.

FISHING EXPEDITION

Went fishing today.

Tried to catch a poem,

Hoping to pull one

Out of the water

But none were biting.

All I caught was

A couple of platitudes.

They weren't worth much

So I threw them back in.

NO BED OF ROSES

"Life is not a bed of roses"
So goes the old saying.
I appreciate the sentiment

But after trimming the rose bushes
In our yard
I've concluded that
        while rose blossoms
        in their various colors
        are a treat for the eyes
        their stems are another matter.

The bushes in our yard
Range from prickly
To mean as hell.
They send out statements like
"Don't get too close" and
"Keep out"

So I respected their warnings
By wearing a pair of gloves
And concluding that roses
Are things of beauty
But I couldn't rest peacefully
On a bed of them.

FOR MY MOTHER

My mother died at age sixty-two,
When I was almost twenty- three.
Recently, while doing some housecleaning,
my wife discovered a picture of her,
a twenty-five year old bride
carrying a bouquet of lilies of the valley.

Who could have guessed that pretty
young woman had such a well of wisdom
and humor and love within her?

Who, looking at this picture,
would have known how forgiving
she would turn out to be to the last of her
five children, her late blooming son, tied up
in his own little world, not yet
able to give back the kind of
love she so consistently offered?

Yet somehow I feel sure she would have
both forgiven and truly forgotten any
worry or pain I had caused her.
The bride in this picture,
        grown older, her hair almost white,
        seemed to have cancelled my debts
        in advance and would wonder
        what on earth I was talking about.

EMPTYING THE TRASH

It's my duty and privilege
to gather the trash
at least two times a week.

Doesn't call for much thought.
It has a certain rhythm
as I empty the wastebaskets
into a large black plastic bag
which goes into a container
in the shed.

Sometimes, when proceeding
through this ritual,
I whistle or sing
a little off key

wishing it were as easy
to dump out
those useless odds and ends
that rattle around
in my head.

AGENDA

Today, before leaving the house,
my wife asked me if I had time
to wash the floors in the kitchen
and bathroom.

I have some thoughts of what I'd
like to do today – namely write,
work out at the exercise center,
eat lunch at Panera's and
take a nap.

But my little black appointment book
is a blank for this date.
Nothing in it to prevent me from
washing those floors.
So I told her I'd try
to fit that job in between
my various commitments.

Better get at it. Looks like a full
day ahead!

VANITY

What's wrong with being wrong?
Must we always be right?
Do we wish to set a record
of rightness and for that reason
can't make mistakes?

I wonder about that,
in regard to myself and others.

Is admitting you were wrong
the end of an unblemished
record?

or a step
in the right direction,
learning something,
becoming like others,
sometimes right, sometimes not.
Forget about records.

HAND WRINGING

I'm discovering after a good deal of
thinking that the most useless activity
I can imagine is hand wringing –
deploring this and bemoaning that,
shaking one's head and declaring
things are not like they used to be
the world is a mess, the neighbors
unfriendly, the tide is against us,
had a string of bad luck.
but why act like a victim when
some things can be fixed and
seeds can be planted and
sunsets, sunrises and unexpected
kindnesses remind us that
life is a gift.

SLOWING DOWN

It comes naturally.
You don't have to work at it.
Getting older takes care of it.

When I was young and middle aged,
I'd look at someone older
And say to myself "He's so slow!"
"Why does it take him so long
To pocket his change,
Get out of the way?"

> May God forgive my earlier impatience!
> It's dawned on me that I am he.

EARLY MEMORY

Couldn't have been more than
two or three years old
at the time.

A woman whom I'll call
Ms. G
was taking care of me.

I remember walking with
Ms. G in the woods and
looking out at a lake.

We stopped while I
 picked up a pine cone
 and she sat on a log.

As I looked over at her
she smiled reassuringly.
That smile

still warms my heart,
as though she were saying
"You're ok by me."

Belated thanks, Ms. G.

WHAT'S WRONG WITH GOATS?

How did goats get such a bad rap, as
in "separate the sheep from the goats"
with the goats losing out
in the last judgment?

But why? What did they do
to offend the judge?
Is it because sheep are docile
and goats stubborn

or eat with less discrimination?
Must be some history
to this goat prejudice.
People talk about scapegoats.
Never heard of a scapesheep.
It isn't even a word.

LISTENING

Time spent listening is,
I think, on the whole,
time well spent.
Unless you feel there
is nothing out there
that you need to hear.

Listening comes in
various forms such as
listening to music or
to a story of something
that happened yesterday
or 2,500 years ago.

It takes work, that is
if you're paying attention
and not day- dreaming or
wondering: "When is this
person going to

stop talking so I can
say something
more interesting?"

It's possible to listen
when no one is talking,
the only sounds
a singing bird, a
dog barking, even
no sound at all.

SET APART

There's something in us
that wants to be
set apart
from other people.

More accomplished
than those who surround us.
More righteous
than the run of the mill.

It makes us feel better
to think we inhabit
a finer type planet.

But sooner or later
our planet feels lonely.
Nobody to talk to
so we talk to ourselves
which soon becomes
as boring as hell.

It's not what it's cracked
up to be, this lofty planet.
Better go back to where
we belong, claim a spot
as one among many
and discover we're a lot
like them and they,
surprisingly, like us.

SPACEY THOUGHTS

From time to time
one hears stories
of how human beings
are conquering space.

Which may mean
going more quickly
from one place
to another.

Even from earth
to the moon.
Or sending a device
to land on Mars.

But how in the world
does one conquer space
when it appears
there's an unlimited
supply of it?

It's like saying you've
conquered air.
Space is like air.
It's just there.

Can I say I conquered
two miles of space
after walking to Asylum
Avenue and back?

The test of a journey
to most anywhere
is not what you've conquered.
It's what you've discovered
between here and there.

WHAT AND WHERE

What are conservatives

conserving?

Where are progressives

progressing?

Do labels define us

or, quite often,

confuse us?

LESSER GODS

What is it that keeps people apart these days,
that prevents our civil debate from being civil?
Why do we call one another fools and idiots and
use other terms that are rather unprintable?

It seems like in the good old ship U S of A
we who live side by side often inhabit different
planets. "Government" – for some is
an entity that should get out of the way.

It is evil per se. For others it ensures
fair play. Freedom is a beautiful word
to which we all adhere but means quite
different things to different ears.

Have we lost our moorings, our sense of
connection? What's wrong with us as a
nation? What makes us so cranky and
uncivil to put it mildly? What makes us talk

so wildly? What are we afraid of?
Maybe what's needed is to find what we've
lost, a sense of belonging to something
greater that brings us together.

WASHING THE DISHES

There's something therapeutic about washing
dishes. It makes me feel good to clean up
the kitchen after eating a supper
cooked by my spouse.

I like to wipe off the counters,
rinse off the plates
and load up the dishwasher
while shifting my mind into neutral.

You can think of anything or nothing
at all. I might whistle or sing
or wonder about the weather
while scrubbing a pan.

This activity connects me to my
father who used to wash dishes
without help from a dishwasher.
I feel part of a succession of people.

In a world that's uncertain
dishwashing is a tangible thing.
Take a look at that counter, I say.
It looks a lot better.

NOT PREDICTABLE

Poems, I'm slowly discovering,
Are not predictable.
They acquire a life of
Their own, going in a different
Direction, not ending up
Where you thought
They would or should.
They are like some people
You thought you knew well
Who turn out to be full of
Surprises.
So fasten your seat belt
If you're writing a poem.

WHY?

Children ask that question
All the time.

Why do I have to go to bed
 So early?
– Why do dogs bark?
– Why do stars come out
  At night?
– Why did my goldfish die?

Some of these questions
Are easy to answer
But after a while they get us in
Over our heads
And the only available answer is
"I don't know"

So, instead of offering
Unconvincing explanations
For all those deep "why" questions,

I went out and bought
Twenty pounds of birdseed.
Don't ask me why.

PART THREE

CREDO

CREDO

As a very late contributor
to the world of poetry
I can hardly believe
I'm writing these verses.
What has gotten into you?
I say to myself.
What is it that pushes you
to write poems at four score
and more?
Darned if I know.

Perhaps it's a way of
saying the down to earth and
the holy make a good fit and
reverence and irreverence can
get along well.

That, in the midst of it all,
the pain and the sorrow,
the unanswerable questions,
there's a kind of harmony
and a love that doesn't let go.

BELIEVING

According to some who've
Thought about the matter
The opposite of faith is not doubt.
It's certainty.

If all questions of life and death
Can be wrapped up
In a container
What room remains for mystery?
Or anything that doesn't fit?

To declare doubt and faith opposites
Is like saying winter and spring have
No connection
And what you can't see isn't there.
But faith, according to one scripture
Writer, is evidence of things
unseen.

No airtight case for God
Provable in a court of law
Has been provided.
Only stories
Of lost people found,
Homecomings
And broken things mended.

PAY ATTENTION

It's a simple piece of advice.

Sounds like something

Your fifth grade teacher

Might have told her class.

Do you ever outgrow

The need to hear it?

I doubt it.

BOOMERANG

When I think of Australia,
a country I haven't seen
or expect to see,
several images come to mind,

one of which is an invention
called the boomerang.

You throw it out
and it comes back to you.

Comparisons are odious,
the saying goes.

So when I set about
comparing myself

to the detriment
of somebody else,

I try to remember
to duck my head,
even lie flat on the ground,

because I've just thrown
a boomerang and it's
coming back at me!

SACRED PLACES

A little past ten o'clock on
a Sunday morning outside
Center Church in downtown
Hartford, Connecticut.

The small portable table
where coffee, hot chocolate and
granola bars are served
has been taken back into the church.

Hundreds of pigeons, all appearing
well fed,
congregate on the sidewalk,
busy picking up pieces of bread.

People sitting on the church steps,
some homeless, some just resting
or waiting for their bus
to come by.

Now and then somebody
getting up and going
inside – settling into a pew,
praying, getting warm.

The choir assembling at the
back of the church, ready for
the start of the service.

Seems like the God,
worshiped inside,
is also out here.

BENEDICTION

It means "good word" and is what
often concludes a service of worship
or some sort of public event.

The idea being that such gatherings
should end on a positive note
with some word of hope.

But people can be benedictions
I think, people like Jane, who
lived to be nearly a hundred and four.

She was out and about for almost
all of her life, though I only knew
her the last twenty seven

of those years. It cheered you up
to just be around her. All summer
long she'd bring flowers to church

from her son's garden. She wrote
letters, it seemed by the bushel, to
hundreds of people on all sorts

of occasions or no occasion at all
saying things like thanks, keep at it,
congratulations or what do you think

of that? Jane kept on going until she
was gone, at least from our sight.
Never a large person, she appeared

to occupy less space as
she grew older. But it's a strange
sort of thing I cannot explain about

Jane but I swear it is true. As there was less of her there seemed to be more of her.

CERTAINTY

Recently, it's become clear to me
that some who speak with certainty
on a variety of matters, may not be
as sure of themselves as they
appear to be.

Those who talk most vehemently
advocating one position or another
may later share their doubts about
their earlier certitudes and say that
they were wrong.

Consider Judge Samuel Sewell of the
Salem Witch Trial fame. He might have
had an inkling he made a bad decision,
when later he became an advocate for
the rights of women.

BALANCING ACT

Keeping your balance
is like
learning to ride
a bicycle

and discovering
by trial and error
how not to fall off
on one side
or the other
while moving ahead.

Such as falling for
a sure fire remedy
promising to cure
whatever ails you
or the world

And then becoming
a certified cynic
declaring there's nothing
that can make a
bad situation even
a little bit better.

Keep moving,
but not so fast
that you don't know
where you are heading
seems to be good advice.

A lesson that someday
I hope to learn, perhaps
at age one hundred
and seventy- five.

AT AGE 81

One thing is sure
I'm not going to die young
As Wendell Berry said
At the tender age of 70.
No predicting the future.
No use dwelling on the past.

Live for today
Keep your eyes open,
Your ears too
Even though, in my case,
You don't hear very well.

Make appointments
But no more five year goals
Or things of that sort.
A year or two is enough.
Laugh at yourself.

Enjoy being thought wise
When you know
That you aren't.
Eat what you want
Say thanks from the heart.

And try to be nice.

BUSY

"It's good to be busy" the old adage goes.
Look at the bees, we're told.
See how busy they are.
Take a lesson from them.

Surely there are things to be learned
from those industrious bees.
You cannot help
but applaud them.

But is it a waste of time to be idle,
to look at the trees
and the sky and people going by
or stare into space?

Must I rush through life
as though it's a race,
quite often missing what's
in front of my face?

ASSISTED LIVING

As used now, "assisted living" is
a technical term applied to
people who need help getting through
the day and who, without such
assistance, might become confused
and, in some cases, wander away not
knowing where they were going.

Might that be too restrictive a definition?
Who among us knows exactly
where she or he is heading and needs
no assistance in finding their way?
No parent, no mentor, no teacher, no
doctor, no friend, no elder, no listener?
No one to stand by and cheer, or perhaps
tell you to wait a minute or give you a
kick in the rear?

I can't imagine anyone of any age
not needing assistance. What nonsense!
What foolishness even to think you
can go it alone! So thanks to all the
assisters who have become a part of my
life – my parents, my children, my wife–
and to X, Y and Z, among
others. All told, too many to count.

SAID AND UNSAID

Words have a great many uses.
They can encourage, explain,
proclaim, tell stories,
do all sorts of things.

Such as getting caught up
on the events of the day,
or the new people who
moved in next door.

Words, known as instructions,
can help you assemble a
device just brought home
from the store.

But sometimes words can't
accomplish what you wish
they would.

Only a hug, something to eat
or standing around, not
knowing what to say,
will do.

LENT

A season to remember
we're not here forever.

Time set aside to ponder
what Jesus did
and went through
to help us see God
more clearly

and discover
what it means
to love one another.

EASTER

Another Easter, arriving on time
according to the vagaries
of the Gregorian calendar.

Words like resurrection,
spring, new life.
All trying to describe
an event

that goes beyond telling
yet needs to be told
about someone named Jesus

Who I don't see as
placating an offended Deity
on our behalf

But as God's way
of reaching out and
showing slow learners
like you and me

Who God was and is
and always will be
and helping blind folks
to see.

EMPTY SPACES

There's something appealing
about empty spaces

such as deserts, blue skies,
early morning quiet. They're
like blank sheets of paper.

No hurry to fill up those
spaces with sounds or opinions.
Let them be for a while.

Something will emerge from
them unbidden, a way ahead
open up more clearly.

God, we're often reminded,
speaks in empty spaces.

EXTRAORDINARY

What's wrong with being
Ordinary?
Head of this. Best of that.
As though life were some
Sort of contest.
Most popular,
Most successful,
Smartest,
Strongest,
Busiest,
Funniest.
I have a fantasy
Of someone climbing
On a stage and
Proclaiming
To whoever will listen,
I'm opting out
Of the system.
I've no number at all.
Please don't put me
On your list.

FINDING YOUR VOICE

Unless they have laryngitis,
it doesn't seem to be a problem
for animals to find their voice. It's
natural for a dog to bark and
for birds to sing the songs
allotted to their species.

For us humans finding your voice
is a different thing.
It's more a matter of saying
what you want to say,
conveying to others
what you wish to convey.

Some find their voice in fixing
broken things, like cars and lawnmowers.
Some in writing, painting, cooking,
helping the neighbors
or making people laugh.

There are things inside us
yearning to emerge
and order any obstacles to
get out of the way.

"I DON'T KNOW"

These words,
carved into a piece of wood,
made me smile.
I found the honesty refreshing.

Seems to be no shortage
of answer people,
quick to declare how to

– fix the economy
– make money
– improve your marriage
– lose weight
– get right with God

No time for questions.
No room for doubt.
No place for mystery.

Makes you want to go out
and get some fresh air.

Saying "I don't know"
might make it possible

to learn something
you didn't know before.

OFFERING

I'm not interested in long explanations
of what some people call the Eucharist,
others Communion.

But today in church, as the minister
 led the congregation in familiar words
inviting all to the table, it felt as though

no one was left out. While I know the
Eucharist is a Christian sacrament of
thanksgiving for what Jesus revealed of God

it seemed that the bread and
(in our case) Welch's grape juice were
a reminder to people of every religion

or no religion that God is found
in down to earth events – as when you eat,
celebrate a graduation, mourn the loss of a

friend, feel alone. The bread and cup seemed
to tell of a love offered to each and to all –
an offering that always surprises.

RELUCTANT LEARNERS

(by one)

Jesus spoke of becoming like a child.
Buddhists recommend a beginners mind.

I have come to the conclusion that
We human beings learn reluctantly,
Mostly in bits and pieces. It happens when
People open the doors of their minds
At least a crack

And confess:
"Can you help me fix this thing?"
"I don't know what to say."
"How can I get from here to there?"
"Why do people treat each other that way?"

It's very difficult, almost impossible,
To learn something with a "do not disturb"
Sign on the door of your mind.

RHYTHM

Used to think
Some people had rhythm,
Others didn't.
As simple as that.

Now it's becoming clear that
Everybody has.
It's a matter of listening to the music
And following the beat.

Farmers know the rhythm of
Seedtime and harvest,
Daylight and darkness,
Sunshine and rain.

So do those who've known
Sorrows and joys,
Gains and losses,
One after another.

Which includes everyone
Who's lived long enough.
All God's children,
I think.

FITTING IN

Nobody wants to be considered
    – a square peg in a round hole
    – a fifth wheel
    – or, God forbid, a misfit.

It's not a bad thing
To want to fit in
To a group or society
Of which there are
Many varieties.

But the kind of belonging
To which I mostly aspire
Is one where none are excluded.
No ins or outs.
No one higher or lower,

Where all that's required
Is to find the space
That's waiting for you
And then
Try to fill it.

SABBATHS

A Sabbath, whatever the day or the hour,
Is time set apart
To be reminded
Of things forgotten
Or never known.

Time to picture a way of living
Where the first
Shall be last and
The meek
Inherit the earth.

Time to see through illusions
Of money and power
And laugh at pretenses,
Both our own
And others.

To view with new eyes
The world around and within.
Time to remember
The One who made us.

Observing a Sabbath
Turns the tables on everything.

SOMETHING MORE

It seems every poet worth his or her salt
must write at least one poem
and preferably quite a few touching
on the subject of our mortality and how,
sooner or later, we all turn to dust.

It's very mysterious, this living and dying.
Life leads to death and death to life. I'd like
to package an answer explaining how this
happens. But answers come mostly in bits and
pieces, in stories from scriptures

and from accounts of so called "thin places"
where the world of eating and drinking,
peacemaking, lovemaking, grieving and
trying to make ends meet come close to another
world, almost within reach,

where fair play and justice, kindness and hope
and an unbidden love seem to reach out
amazingly, gracefully. Something more
than we could have formulated in creeds
or in lists of things we are told to believe.

STUMBLING

I must confess to a certain envy of those who
navigate their way through life smoothly.
Who know by some sort of instinct
who they are and where they're going.

Who set goals and reach them, go from strength
to strength, starting right out of the box and
never look back. Who are successful and useful
and move only forward, year after year after year.

But closer inspection shows, for most folks
at least, this isn't the case. It's a step or two
forward, then a step or two back.
Going down a blind alley and then starting over.

Saying things you wish you hadn't. Not
saying things you wish you had. Missing what's
in front of you. Realizing it's too late to say
I'm sorry to someone you've hurt.

But sometimes, for whatever the reason, the sky
becomes clearer. If all is not gained, all is not lost
either. By God's grace, I know no other way to
say it, you've stumbled toward a better place.

YOU MUST

Be born again, the preacher said.
Here's how you go about it.
He looked sincere but
Like somebody needing
To separate
The ins from the outs.

Born again? Does
That make you an insider,
Set apart?
Or is it coming home
And, to your surprise,
Being welcomed on the way?

The preacher didn't say.

UNFINISHED BUSINESS

However long a person has been
on this earth, can he or she claim to
have no unfinished business?
Can all the loose ends be tied together,
ever? Not as far as I can see.
Jobs not yet done, words unsaid,
plenty to learn or unlearn, surprises
popping up at each bend of the road.
Getting everything all wrapped
up may be a laudable goal
but one quite unattainable
when we ourselves are
unfinished business.

RECOVERING

One should not be ashamed of
being in a state of recovery.
It seems like everybody is
or needs to be,
whether this condition or
affliction can be medically
described or not.

You don't have to be
a certified member
of a recovery group
to know you're in a ditch
and can't get out
or have wandered off
somewhere with no idea
how to get back.

That's why those who pray
"God help us" most often
speak from the heart.

Recovering may reveal illusions
and make us feel foolish.
But at least it's better
to be recovering from what ails us
than coming down with it!

DARKNESS AND LIGHT

The book of Genesis,
meaning beginnings,
says each day of creation
included both darkness and light,
night and day.

The gospel according to John
declares that darkness
can't put out the light.

Photographers often
use the contrast
when they take pictures
like the one I saw

showing bright sunlight
shining through spaces
between the dark boards of a barn.

Darkness appears to just
sit there.
It doesn't go anywhere.

Light takes the initiative,
going everywhere.
The business of light
is to shine.

SET FREE

Liberty is a word
that calls for a celebration.

It's the fourth of July
with fireworks bursting
into showers, every color
of the rainbow.

It's walls falling:
The walls of Jericho
tumbling down.
The Berlin wall no longer
severing a City.

It's a Statue of Liberty,
her torch held high.

It's singing We Shall Overcome
and no longer sitting
in the back of the bus.

It's Isaiah and Jesus proclaiming
release to the captives.

It's the Hallelujah Chorus.

It's people set free to become
What they were meant to be.

I AM

Time may not fly
But it doesn't hold still.
Try to grab a moment
And it slips through your fingers.

Seems like everything changes
So we look for something
That doesn't go by,
Wear out or spoil.

When Moses came down
From Mt. Sinai,
He announced that God's name
Was "I am."
Not "I was" or "I will be."

Present in the midst
Of coming and going,
Celebrating and mourning.
Unbounded by time.
Simply, "I am."

About the Poet

Van Parker is a United Church of Christ Minister and Minister Emeritus of the First Church in Windsor, Connecticut (U.C.C.) where he served as Pastor for 27 years. Since retirement he has spent his time volunteering, growing vegetables, writing articles and reflections and, more recently, poems.

He and his wife Lucille divide their time between their home in Danville, Vermont and an apartment in West Hartford, Connecticut. They have three children and seven grandchildren.

This is Van's first book of poetry. His works have previously appeared in magazines and newspapers.

CPSIA information can be obtained at www.ICGtesting.com
Printed in the USA
LVOW132156170912

299231LV00012B/40/P

9 781936 711215